JAMES DEAN

JAMES DEAN

The Untold Story of a Passion for Speed

Philippe Defechereux
Jean Graton

© GRATON ÉDITEUR S.A. 1995 All rights reserved.
© MEDIAVISION PUBLICATIONS, INC. 1996 for the English version.
Published in 1995 in French under the title,
James Dean—La Passion Foudroyée by Graton Éditeur S.A., Brussels, Belgium.

No part of this book may be reproduced or utilized in any form or by any means, electronic or mechanical, including photocopying, recording or by any information storage and retrieval system, without the written permission of Mediavision Publications Inc., which may be contacted at the following address:

Mediavision Publications, Inc.
9200 Sunset Blvd., Suite 404
Los Angeles, California 90069
USA

ISBN:
0-9651380-4-6
[ISBN for the Graton Éditeur S.A. edition, James Dean—La Passion Foudroyée: 2-87098-024-8]

PREMIUM EDITION

PRODUCTION CREDITS

Translation	Intex Translations
English Editor	Nancy Boss Art
French Editor	Philippe Graton
Cover Design	Jamie Pfeifer
Book Design (French)	Dominique Chantrenne
Legal Counsel	Rogers & Harris
Pre-Press Production	Groupe G/Tallon (Belgium)
Cover Separations	Separacolor International
Printer	World Wide Graphics, Inc.
Project Supervisor	Godfrey Harris

PHOTO AND ILLUSTRATION CREDITS

Cover	Sanford Roth (?)	©David Loehr Collection	Page 16 (Clipped Pages)	Motoracing Magazine (Vol 1, No. 8, 9)	Courtesy Jim Sitz
Page 7	Doc Delange	©Stills/Sénépart	Page 16 (Photos, L-R)	East of Eden	©Cinestar/Sénépart
Page 8 (top)	Unknown	©Nelva Jean Thomas		Rebel With a Cause	©Nadia/Sénépart
Page 8 (bottom)	Unknown	©London Features/Sénépart		Giant	©Shooting Star/Van Parys
Page 9 (top)	Dennis Stock	©Magnum Photos	Page 17	Gus Vignolle (?)	©David Loehr Collection
Page 9 (bottom)	Unknown	©Marcus Winslow	Page 36-37	Sanford Roth	©Seita Ohnishi
Page 10 (center)	Unkonwn	©London Features/Sénépart	Page 38	Sanford Roth	©London Features/Sénépart
Page 11	Dennis Stock	©Magnum Photos	Page 39 (top)	Sanford Roth (?)	©London Features/Sénépart
Page 12/13 (top)	Sanford Roth	©Seita Ohnishi	Page 39 (bottom)	Unknown	©David Loehr Collection
Page 12 (bottom)	Sanford Roth	©Seita Ohnishi	Page 40	Unknown	©David Loehr Collection
Page 13 (bottom)	Unknown	©London Features/Sénépart	Page 48	Sanford Roth	©Seita Ohnishi
Page 14 (top/middle)	Sanford Roth	©Seita Ohnishi	Page 49 (top)	Sanford Roth	©Seita Ohnishi
Page 14 (film strip)	Unknown	©Lee Raskin	Page 49 (bottom)	Film National Safety Council	©Archive Films
Page 15 (top)	Rebel Without a Cause	©Sygma/Van Parys	Page 50	Unknown	©Seita Ohnishi
Page 15 (right)	Gus Vignolle (?)	©David Loehr Collection			

PRINTED IN THE UNITED STATES OF AMERICA

TABLE OF CONTENTS

7
One-Speed Jimmy

17
A Word from Michael Valliant

21
James Dean's Three Races

36
A Passion for Speed

41
James Dean's Last Day

48
The Truth Reconstructed

50
Michael Valliant's Opinion

51
The Porsches of James Dean

52
Acknowledgements
Bibliography

One-Speed Jimmy

One important aspect of James Dean's life has always remained obscure: the nature and extent of his passion for racing cars. Still not used to his stardom, the young man from rural Indiana felt uncomfortable in the high-powered circles of Hollywood. Motorbikes and fast cars allowed Jimmy to stay in touch with the way he grew up. Speed and the mastery of driving gave him a true sense of self—and freedom.

James Byron Dean was born on February 8, 1931 in the small town of Marion, Indiana. Soon, thereafter, the family moved to nearby Fairmount. From the time he was quite young, Jimmy's mother introduced him to the artistic forms of life, specially music, dance and theater. In 1936, his father, a dental technician, was offered an attractive job in California, and, so, the

Jimmy at 17 in Fairmount on his Czech motorbike.

Jimmy's Senior Class Yearbook photo.

young family packed its bags for Los Angeles, leaving behind the Indiana countryside. In Los Angeles at the age of five, Jimmy's life was calm, happy and comfortable. But this would last only until fate intervened.

Orphan at Nine

Jimmy's adored mother fell ill from cancer in the early part of 1940. Her illness progressed rapidly, and she died on July 14, at the age of 29, leaving her nine-year-old son traumatized. In the train that carried her coffin on the long journey back to Indiana, the blond boy ran to the special car at every stop to make sure his mother was still there. For the rest of his life, Jimmy would seek her reassuring presence in vain.

A few days after her funeral, the family decided that Jimmy would stay in Fairmount, Indiana. Mildred's sister, Ortense, and her husband, Marcus, offered to raise Jimmy in the familiar environment of his home town. Ortense and Marcus had always cared deeply for Jimmy and would provide for him lovingly. Winton Dean, Jimmy's father, easily accepted the proposition.

Thus, in a little over a week, the deeply saddened Jimmy found himself an orphan and back on the quiet plains of Indiana. Yet something in him had changed. For four years he had breathed the air of California and often found himself contemplating the inspiring immensity of the Pacific Ocean.

Soon, Jimmy started dreaming big dreams, vowing to overcome his fate and to forge his own destiny. He would become a famous actor, hoping to get from the public the unconditional love and limitless affection his mother could no longer give him. He would do everything, try everything, even push back the limits of the possible, to get there.

A Thirst for Action

Following his mother's inspiration and encouraged by Ortense, Jimmy began his quest by studying speech and drama. At Fairmount High, he had the good fortune of being tutored by Adeline Nall, an influential drama and speech teacher. Quickly refining his acting skills, James Dean was selected in 1946 to make his public acting debut at the age of 15. He was ecstatic. He took part in all the plays put on by his school. His progress was so impressive that in 1949 he was selected to represent the State of Indiana in a national speakers' competition. He managed to advance as far as the semifinals, finishing in sixth place overall.

But acting was not enough for this young man brimming with energy and thirsting for action. Though nearsighted and therefore forced to wear glasses, he managed to become an accomplished athlete, equally at ease on basketball courts and baseball diamonds. But the passion churning inside him was deeper than some sports could fulfill. It was a passion he had felt since he was 15—ever since he had received a small American motorbike, called a Whizzer, as a gift from his Uncle Marcus.

Jimmy raced it after hours, getting his first taste of speed and horsepower. Always looking for the most challenging roads he could find, he would try every bend full speed, endlessly attempting to cut a tighter and faster line through it. In so doing, he discovered that driving, like theater, is an art.

Awesome Stunts

A gifted driver by nature, Jimmy soon discovered the limitations of his first bike. His Uncle Marcus realized this and bought him a brand new, Czechoslovakian motorbike, called a "Czech." From the moment he got his "real bike," Jimmy spent long evenings in Marvin Carter's shop where his uncle had purchased the bike. There he not only studied mechanics, but also how to ride his new bike, rapidly mastering the new machine. He managed to perform awesome stunts effortlessly, like flattening himself on the seat while running the Czech flat out at 50 mph. His Uncle Marcus would later recall: "He never got hurt, and he never found anything he couldn't do well almost the first time he tried it. Just one fall off the bike and he would have been afraid of speed, but he was without fear."

From Two Wheels to Four

Cars came next. The first one Jimmy tried was a friend's souped-up 1934 Plymouth, which the owner occasionally allowed his close friends to take turns driving. On certain weekends, the group would test its members on a dirt road with a tight S-turn

On a visit to Fairmount, Jimmy shares his passion with his cousin Markie. The model is a Jaguar XK-120.

The corner of the photo below has been enlarged to show the only existing picture of James Dean's first car, an MG TD.

on the outskirts of town. The boys called it "Suicide Curve." In little time, Jimmy became the only one who dared go through the curve at top speed, while staying in full control of the car.

One member of the group who tried to match Jimmy's speed ended up doing a stunning somersault, fortunately without injury. Such feats soon earned Jimmy the nickname "One-Speed-Dean." The only speed he knew, Fairmount people said, was flat out.

Yet on June 14, 1949, only two weeks after graduating from Fairmount High, Jimmy gave up his machines for what he hoped would be a career in acting. He moved to California, welcomed by his father and new stepmother. His intention was to enroll in acting classes at UCLA, even though Winton Dean clearly expressed his wish to see his son become a lawyer. Eventually, Jimmy had his way. Within a year, he was chosen to play Malcolm in a version of Macbeth staged by the University.

Riding a Norton In New York

In December of 1950, Jimmy hired an agent. Gradually, he began to get a few minor commercial roles, including one for Pepsi Cola. But failing to get a bigger break in the ensuing months, he decided to move to New York. Broadway theaters were then considered a perfect launching pad for talented actors with big dreams about Hollywood but who lacked contacts there. Though always short on money, Jimmy soon found a friend nice enough to lend him a Norton motorcycle. He was seen racing through the New York streets as fast as he used to race through the little country roads around Fairmount. Most of his friends quickly shied away from riding with him. Yet, he never had an accident.

In New York, Jimmy was gradually able to secure roles in a number of television series. Then he was cast in two Broadway plays: *See The Jaguar* and *The Immoralist*, the latter adapted from a novel by André Gide, where he co-starred with Geraldine Page and Louis Jourdan. While neither play gained much public attention, they revealed the young actor's ability to a few directors in search of new talent. One of them was Elia Kazan, already famous for his gripping movie, *On The Waterfront*, starring Marlon Brando.

At the time, Kazan was looking for a new young actor to star in *East of Eden*, his next film with Warner Brothers.

On February 16, 1954, Kazan gave Jimmy an audition at Warner Brothers' New York offices on 44th Street.

Three weeks later, James Dean was on a plane for Hollywood; by April 7, he had signed his first contract with Warner. Like a champion, Jimmy had just vaulted himself to success.

"Nobody tells me what to do..."

From the moment he returned to California, James Dean's passion for speed intensified. In the Spring of 1954, he spent his first movie actor's wages on a secondhand Triumph T-110 motorcycle. His selection of this bike was hardly accidental; it was inspired by Jimmy's idol, Marlon Brando. Brando, who was 7 years older than Dean, had gained stardom with the opening in 1948 of *A Streetcar Named Desire*.

And in a 1954 film, *The Wild One*, Brando had played the role of a motorcycle gang leader who challenged the establishment astride a Triumph.

There was a line in the film that defined Brando's character: "Nobody tells me what to do..." Jimmy identified with those words.

As soon as he could afford it, Jimmy traded in his road bike for a new Triumph T-500, which was more powerful than the previous model.

His favorite pastime was to persuade a friend or date to mount the bike behind him, and then to terrorize them by racing "flat-out" through the hairpin corners of Hollywood's canyons.

In May of the same year, just before star-

In the photo on the facing page, Jimmy, cousin Markie, and a "Special" are seen in Fairmount in February 1955.
(Photo Dennis Stock
© Magnum Photos)

James Dean gets to know his first Porsche.

© 1987 Seita Ohnishi; Photo by Sanford Roth

ting to shoot his first film, Jimmy made the leap. He bought a car, a red MG TD—naturally, a sports car. While it wasn't too expensive, it had a peppy engine. This English two-seater had become one of the first European sports cars to attract significant numbers of Americans. During this period, Detroit's automobile industry wasn't building race cars or many sports cars, deferring this new market to the Europeans. American auto makers preferred to build big ostentatious cars, without paying too much attention to their road handling or braking capability. They were mainly interested in things like comfort, gadgets, and chrome. The choice for driving enthusiasts among domestic products was thus narrowly limited to a hodgepodge of homemade "specials" or upgraded one-of-a-kind hot rods.

these European thoroughbreds. From coast to coast, the sporting aficionados' cars of choice were such names as MG, Porsche, Triumph, Jaguar, and Ferrari.

Drivers of these cars began to win consistently on road racing circuits, just as sports car racing, popular in Europe since the beginning of the century, began to take hold in America.

Jimmy had been keen on European machines from the time of his early motorcycles. His new Porsche was thus a natural choice. A clean white convertible, it had a 1.5 cylinder "racing" engine and 70 hp, giving the car a top speed of 100 miles per hour (160 km/h).

This model was called the Speedster S in the United States, and it became the perfect stepping stone for amateur racers who wanted to learn while winning. In the "under 1500cc" class, the Speedster S was a sure winner for drivers who could control the car's tendency to oversteer.

"Rebel Without a Cause"

The script he was reading at the time he bought the Speedster S, *Rebel Without a Cause*, undoubtedly heightened Jimmy's desire for a faster car. In one of the film's critical moments, two young hot rod rivals battle it out. Jim (played by Jimmy) and gang leader Buzz (played by Corey Allen) compete for the heart of Judy (Natalie Wood).

They take off neck and neck, forging ahead flat out toward a sea cliff. The first driver to bail out of his car before going over the cliff would be the "chicken," losing face in front of his peers and Judy. Before climbing into his 1946 Ford, Jim slipped on an open front red nylon windbreaker, his favorite. Buzz wore his usual black leather jacket. As Judy and the gang members looked on, the two cars lunged toward the drop-off. At the last moment, Jim jumped off to safety, but Buzz, having caught the sleeve of his jacket in the door handle, failed to bail out in time.

His Girlfriend Has Competition

Jimmy's delight with his new car was expressed to Barbara Glenn, his girlfriend in New York, to whom he wrote: "Honey!!! A new addition has been added to the Dean family. I got a red 53, MG (milled head etc. hot engine). My sex pours itself into fast curves, broadslides and broodings; drags, etc. You have plenty of competition now. My motorcycle, my MG and my girl. I have been sleeping with my M.G. We make it together. /s/HONEY."

Ten months later, after extending his contract with Warner Brothers and signing for his second film, Jimmy traded the MG for a newer and faster sports car, a 356 Porsche convertible. A growing number of American racing enthusiasts were buying and racing

In Bakersfield, Jimmy slides into the car of his dreams-a Ferrari Mondial, belonging to Josie von Neumann, the importer's daughter.

On September 3-4, 1955, James Dean attended the Santa Barbara race, but wasn't allowed to participate in it because he hadn't finished shooting Giant. (Notice his temples, which were shaved for the final scenes of the film.) The Speedster with No. 86 was raced by Dale Johnson.

Amateur film strips showing James Dean in action in Palm Springs.

Trapped by his metal cage, he crashed down onto the rocks at the bottom of the cliff. Following the incident, Judy drew close to Jim.

From the moment Jimmy took the wheel of his responsive little Speedster, he exhibited some of the traits his former Fairmount buddies would have recognized, with Mulholland Drive as his new training ground. Connecting Laurel Canyon in Hollywood to Topanga Canyon in Woodland Hills, this famous, winding, two-lane road stretches nearly 19 miles through the Santa Monica Mountains. Jimmy would streak breathlessly back and forth across this challenging stretch of road at dizzying speeds, clocking 1,000 miles in a single week. As one of his friends said, "Some people thought that he would break his neck, but we didn't worry about him. One thing about Jimmy, he possessed an amazing set of reflexes and his coordination was perfect."

Love in a Porsche

One evening, Jimmy invited Natalie Wood for a drive on Mulholland. After running a stretch with the accelerator floored, he parked his Porsche at the lookout with the most beautiful view of the city stretched out below. With the San Fernando Valley as backdrop, Los Angeles sparkled like a river of diamonds. Jimmy and Natalie were alone... and this time they weren't in a movie.

The next day, Jimmy excitedly called his friends, begging them to join him at the studio for a breakfast, while leaving them with the mysterious words, "It can be done." Lew Bracker, Jimmy's insurance agent, and Joe Hyams, a playwright, met a glowing James Dean at the Warner Brothers cafeteria. He announced that he had traversed a new frontier: "I've found a way to make love in the Speedster. We did the impossible!"

Yet, Dean knew that Natalie Wood had many suitors, including Nick Ray, the director of Rebel Without a Cause, and Dennis Hopper, one of the film's young gang members. To Jimmy, this only increased the importance of his conquest, since he had won the young woman in spite of the competition and with the help of his car, just as in Rebel Without a Cause!

Devil to the Wind

It was 1955, the year of Rock Around the Clock, Maybelline, and, the debut of a young unknown named Elvis Presley. The "rebel" trend had just taken hold, upsetting taboos and social conventions and challenging postwar middle class conformity. James Dean's intense thirst for action and freedom fit right in with the mood of the times to do and try everything, almost at any cost.

By so often going against convention, he would irritate others without realizing it. This increased his sense of alienation, already magnified by the artificiality of Hollywood. That is when he would jump into his Porsche to reconnect with his early experience racing on his bike around Fairmount. That is what made him happiest.

To be sure, Jimmy had reason for spending so many hours racing along Mulholland Drive. He wanted to master the Speedster in preparation for entering his first official race.

When a friend confirmed the date of the race weekend, organized by the California Sports Car Club and held every March in Palm Springs, an excited Jimmy registered right away. This would be his first race on a track! After training for so long on open roads, he would finally be able to test himself against veteran drivers on a real racetrack, making his dream come true before the public and the press. The tight circle of experienced drivers remained unimpressed. For them, stardom was earned on the basis of different criteria than used in Hollywood.

Racetrack Driver

The following pages tell the detailed story of the three races James Dean participated in. These races were the fulfillment of his most intense passion. He loved racing and desperately wanted to prove his driving talent. He had just enough time to show real

Victory in Palm Springs, March 26, 1955

DID YOU KNOW...

Few records exist on the racing career of James Dean. In 1955, the young man with the Porsche was hardly famous. The facts presented here were discovered in the United States, Europe, and Japan. Some of the items have never before been published, such as the photographs at the bottom of page 14. The 8mm amateur motion picture clips are the only filmed images of James Dean on a racetrack!

15

potential, before he died on the way to his fourth race. In the pages that follow you will view these races in a way never before experienced by anyone. This is an extraordinary document, containing images not previously seen on film or television. Alongside James Dean we will relive these unforgettable moments, thanks to the remarkable artistic talents of Jean Graton. But first, let's allow one of Europe's most famous fictional characters, Michael Valliant, to introduce us to the cars and the racetracks of that very special time.

These newspaper pages contain the only known photos of Jimmy Dean racing, and quote Dean's ambition to become a world champion driver.

JAMES DEAN'S THREE FILMS

EAST OF EDEN

Directed by Elia Kazan and released in April 1955. Inspired by John Steinbeck's famous novel. Co-stars were Julie Harris, Raymond Massey, and Richard Davalos. This is the only film of his own work that the actor was able to see in movie theaters before his death.

REBEL WITHOUT A CAUSE

Directed by Nicholas Ray and released in October 1955. Co-stars were Natalie Wood, Sal Mineo and Dennis Hopper. This is undoubtedly James Dean's most famous movie. His intense portrayal of a teenager's struggle with the problems of adulthood is an all-time classic.

GIANT

Directed by George Stevens in 1955 and finally released in November 1956. The main stars were Elizabeth Taylor and Rock Hudson, but James Dean stole the lengthy movie.

A Word from Michael Valliant

Michael Valliant is the fictional hero in some 58 graphic novels. Michael drives the competition cars of his family's automobile factory in Formula One and sports car races around the world. In various adventures, Michael associates with a few unforgettable people and comes into contact with some undesirable characters and their unsavory activities. The mixture of realistic fictional situations—within the context of world famous places, events, and personalities—has made Michael Valliant books enormously popular with readers of all ages around the world.

"Hello, friends! Jimmy Dean entered the circuit at a time when sports car racing was just gaining popularity in the United States. Up to that point, the public had only been interested in oval tracks, like Indianapolis. The idea of small winding courses and road racing were still very new to America.

They were considered amateur events in comparison to the relentless battles waged on famous European circuits by Ferrari, Maserati, Jaguar, Aston Martin, and Mercedes-Benz.

At the time, most American race tracks were laid out on airport runways, which allowed the racers to attain maximum speed without endangering spectators. Most of the courses were on military airports lent by the Strategic Air Command. Opening military enclaves for this unusual pastime was rather unusual. General Curtis Le May, the Commander-in-Chief of the Strategic Air Command, was responsible for this deviation from the normal rules. The general was one of us and shared our passion for this new sport, often racing in his own Allard. While Americans were waiting for permanent road racing circuits to be built in Riverside, Watkins Glen, and Laguna Seca, Le May convinced the Pentagon that this would be a very positive undertaking for the image of the United States Air Force.

Every year, the number of spectators grew, reaching 80,000 on weekends involving major prizes at places like Pebble Beach (Monterey) and Torrey Pines (San Diego)—two winding racetracks running through large private estates.

By 1955, road racing was gaining popularity on both the East and West coasts. Road racing weekends were exuberant and highly competitive affairs. Saturdays saw eight to twelve races where drivers of small-engined cars or production sports cars competed in defined classes.

Those finishing in the top spots would not only get a kiss from the local beauty queen and a trophy, but also the chance to race in one of Sunday's two major races. That was the most coveted prize: the opportunity to race against the "Big Boys" and maybe to display enough talent to gradually become one of them.

All the rising drivers of 1955 had moved up that way. Phil Hill, for instance, had started in a little MG TC in 1946, then performed well in a Jaguar XK 120. At age 25, he was one of the winningest Ferrari drivers in America. Caroll Shelby had begun racing Jaguars and Allards in Texas and had moved up to being part of the official Aston Martin racing team. Ken Miles had first tried his hand in a Frazer Nash back in England and had become the undisputed American champion of the under 1500cc category, driving the speedy special racer he had designed himself, the "Flying Shingle." (See page 20)."

Here are some of the best known racing cars competing on American road circuits in 1955, which James Dean aspired to beat. They are a mixture of American Specials and genuine European sports cars, as the first phase of the "great European-American challenge" was then in full swing. This challenge for national prestige had been initiated five years earlier when Briggs Cunningham fielded two modified Cadillacs in the famous 24-hour Le Mans race, then entered his own American-made cars in the 1951 to 1954 races. This battle pitted two completely different philosophies of car design against one another. The cars from Europe were mostly quick, lightweight, and agile. The American cars, on the other hand, emphasized driver comfort, styling, and large engines. As a result, American racing enthusiasts often fabricated their own machines from standard production parts, which they modified for racing in their own workshops. Major examples of these two types of cars are portrayed below. [Blue banners indicate European-manufactured cars; red banners indicate American-built cars.] Okay, is your helmet on tight? Let's go!

MORGENSEN SPECIAL

The prototypical "backyard special", this racer was the brainchild of Dick Morgensen, an Arizona garage owner and racing enthusiast. First assembled in 1954 out of an odd assortment of spare parts found in Morgensen's Phoenix garage, the Morgensen received a mighty Buick V-8 engine and the gearbox of a 1947 Jaguar for the 1955 season. The car was later sold to Max Balchowsky who transformed it into the legendary and victorious "Ol'Yaller."
BUILDER: Dick Morgensen
ENGINE: 5.3 Liter, V-8 Buick
HORSEPOWER: 215 hp
MAXIMUM SPEED: 105 mph (170 km/h)
CAR ILLUSTRATED: At Palm Springs
OWNED AND DRIVEN BY: Dick Morgensen

FERRARI 750 MONZA

When Ferrari developed the 4-cylinder, 3-liter engine Mondial, it won the 1000 km Monza in its first race. Renamed the Monza 750, it won many races with European drivers, notably at Agadir, Dakar, Hyeres, Tunis, Lisbon, and Nassau. Racers Phil Hill and Ernie McAfee introduced this superb car, designed by Scaglietti, to the American racing circuits.
BUILDER: Ferrari
ENGINE: 600/F1 4-cylinder, 2999cc
HORSEPOWER: 260 hp
MAXIMUM SPEED: 165 mph (264 km/h)
CAR ILLUSTRATED: At Santa Barbara
OWNED BY: Bill Doheny
DRIVEN BY: Ernie McAfee

CABALLO DE HIERRO SPECIAL

This unique-looking "hot rod," whose Spanish name means "Iron Horse," was built in early 1953 by California enthusiast Ak Miller and friend Doug Harrison on a 1950 Ford chassis. True to the spirit of home-built specials, it had an Oldsmobile engine, a Cadillac transmission, and Chrysler brakes, all of which worked amazingly well together. Ak Miller normally drove the car. By 1955, the Caballo was a veteran of two Carrera Panamericana's, having finished 14th in the 1953 Mexican race and 7th the following year.
BUILDER: Akton Miller
ENGINE: 5-liter, V-8 Oldsmobile
HORSEPOWER: 185 hp
MAXIMUM SPEED: 120 MPH (190 km/h)
CAR ILLUSTRATED: At Bakersfield
OWNED AND DRIVEN BY: Akton Miller

DEVIN PANHARD

The French Dyna-Panhard would be the first of several models of this car to race Le Mans during the early 1950s. A few of these cars were brought to the United States where they were refitted as "Specials." One such car was the Devin-Panhard belonging to Jean-Pierre Kunstle, a Swiss living in California. The car's tiny 750cc Panhard engine was souped-up with a powerful compressor, and the fiberglass body, built by specialist Bill Devin, reduced the tiny car's overall weight so it could compete effectively against the 2-liter cars of 1955.
BUILDER: Panhard and Bill Devin
ENGINE: Panhard flat 2-cylinder, 750cc souped-up
HORSEPOWER: Unknown
MAXIMUM SPEED: Unknown
CAR ILLUSTRATED: At Bakersfield
OWNED AND DRIVEN BY: Jean-Pierre Kunstle

KURTISS BUICK 500 S

Frank Kurtis was a prolific American race car designer from 1932 to the early 1960s. Starting with Midgets, he graduated to Indy 500 racers in 1941, and his designs won each year between 1950 and 1955. Kurtis modified the victorious 1952 Indy chassis to create his first sports car for sale to collectors. Called the 500 S, it was built on a simple rail-frame-and-tubes chassis mounted on two solid axles and was capable of accepting most American stock engines of the day. Most popular with the Kurtis chassis in 1955 was the new Buick V-8.
BUILDER: Kurtis Kraft
ENGINE: 5.3 liter V-8 Buick
HORSEPOWER: 220 hp
MAXIMUM SPEED: 120 mph (192 km/h)
CAR ILLUSTRATED: At Palm Springs
OWNED AND DRIVEN BY: Bill Murphy of Culver City, CA

ALFA ROMEO BAT

The Alfa Romeo BAT is an extraordinary styling exercise built around an excellent chassis and drive train combination. Launched in 1953, the basic frame and mechanicals are those of the Alfa Romeo 1900, the first mass production car ever manufactured by the Milanese company. The daring styling was the work of Bertone.
BUILDER: Alfa Romeo
ENGINE: 4-cylinder Alfa Romeo, 1975cc
HORSEPOWER: 115 hp
MAXIMUM SPEED: 135 mph (220 km/h)
CAR ILLUSTRATED: At Palm Springs
OWNED AND DRIVEN BY: Al Williams of San Francisco

BALDWIN SPECIAL MK II

Willis Baldwin was a pioneer builder of the "Specials," that began to appear in 1949. Containing several improvements over its first version, the MK II had superior aerodynamics and an 8-cylinder Mercury engine.
BUILDER: Willis Baldwin
ENGINE: 8-cylinder Mercury, 4.2 liters
HORSEPOWER: 150 hp
MAXIMUM SPEED: 105 mph (170 km/h)
CAR ILLUSTRATED: At Palm Springs
OWNED BY: Ken Simpson of Santa Barbara
DRIVEN BY: Bill Pollack

MG R-1

Ken Miles, who in 1966 would drive a Ford GT-40 at Le Mans to second place, started by driving little MGs in California's early road races. Born in England, Miles emigrated to Los Angeles in 1952 and worked for the MG distributor. Early in 1953, he built this first MG Special with a view to beating the OSCAs and Porsches, which were beginning to win big in Class F (under 1500cc). He succeeded! The R-1, made up mostly of MG and Morris parts, except for its new chassis and aluminum body, proved a big winner in 1953 and 1954.
BUILDER: Ken Miles
ENGINE: 4-cylinder MG, 1466cc
HORSEPOWER: 81 hp
MAXIMUM SPEED: 105 mph (160 km/h)
CAR ILLUSTRATED: At Palm Springs
OWNED AND DRIVEN BY: Cy Yedor

AUSTIN HEALEY 100

Already a racing enthusiast before the war, Donald Healey established his company in 1946 and often raced his own cars, with excellent results. In 1951 he manufactured the Healey Silverstone, which had equal success on both sides of the Atlantic. The following year, Healey began creating a new modern car, based on a very simple chassis and Austin mechanics, but fitted with an attractive aluminum body. His contract with Austin gave rise to the Austin-Healey sports car line, beginning with the 100 model.
BUILDER: Austin Cars/Donald Healey
ENGINE: 4-cylinder Austin, 2660cc
HORSEPOWER: 132 hp
MAXIMUM SPEED: 140 mph (225 km/h)
CAR ILLUSTRATED: At Palm Springs
OWNED AND DRIVEN BY: Rodney Sholtes

FRAZER NASH TARGA FLORIO

The racing car line bearing the name of its developer, Captain Archie Frazer Nash, gained fame thanks to "High Speed," which finished third at the 1949 Le Mans. Renamed "Le Mans Replica," it won other races, notably the 1951 Targa Florio, as well as the 1952 12-hour Sebring. The car quickly became less competitive, in spite of attempts by its manufacturer to fit it with a more modern enclosed body.
BUILDER: A.F.N Ltd.
ENGINE: 4-cylinder Bristol, 1966cc
HORSEPOWER: 132 hp
MAXIMUM SPEED: 135 mph (215 km/h)
CAR ILLUSTRATED: At Palm Springs
OWNED AND DRIVEN BY: Marion Lowe, a woman driver

MG R-2 "FLYING SHINGLE"

In 1954, Ken Miles built the R-2 "Flying Shingle" to stay in the competitive field. Aiming to reduce weight and improve aerodynamics, Miles built a completely new car by designing a new chassis and using newer MG and Morris parts. Until the new Porsche 550 Spyder arrived, the MG R-2 won almost all the races early in the 1955 season. Ken Miles then sold his R-2 and joined the California Porsche dealer, John von Neuman.
BUILDER: Ken Miles
ENGINE: 4-cylinder MG, 1466cc
HORSEPOWER: 84 hp
MAXIMUM SPEED: 115 mph (185 km/h)
CAR ILLUSTRATED: At Palm Springs
OWNED AND DRIVEN BY: Ken Miles

SCARAB

This car appeared on the scene in 1958. Lance Reventlow and Bruce Kessler were the last two people (except for Dean's mechanic Rolf Wütherich) to speak to James Dean, at Blackwell's Corners, shortly before his death. During 1956 and 1957, Reventlow drove European cars until he realized that European racing supremacy could be eclipsed by a car built by America's best engineers. Lance, a young millionaire, created his own company, naming his cars in honor of the Egyptian god of immortality, Scarab. Fitted with 5.6 liter Chevrolet engines, the first three Scarabs appeared at the beginning of 1958 and quickly won several races.
BUILDER: Reventlow Automobiles
ENGINE: Modified V-8 Chevrolet, 5560cc
HORSEPOWER: 365 hp
MAXIMUM SPEED: 175 mph (280 km/h)
CAR ILLUSTRATED: At Riverside, October 1958
OWNED BY: Lance Reventlow
DRIVEN BY: Lance Reventlow

VAILLANTE MARATHON

Created in 1957 by Jean Graton for his Great Challenge and driven from the start by Michael Valliant in the pages of Tintin, this Vaillante would surely have outranked its contemporaries if it had existed on something other than paper.
BUILDER: Vaillante
ENGINE: 3.5 liter, V-8 Vaillante
HORSEPOWER: 285 hp
MAXIMUM SPEED: 155 mph (250 km/h)
CAR ILLUSTRATED: By Jean Graton
OWNED BY: Vaillante
DRIVEN BY: Michael Valliant

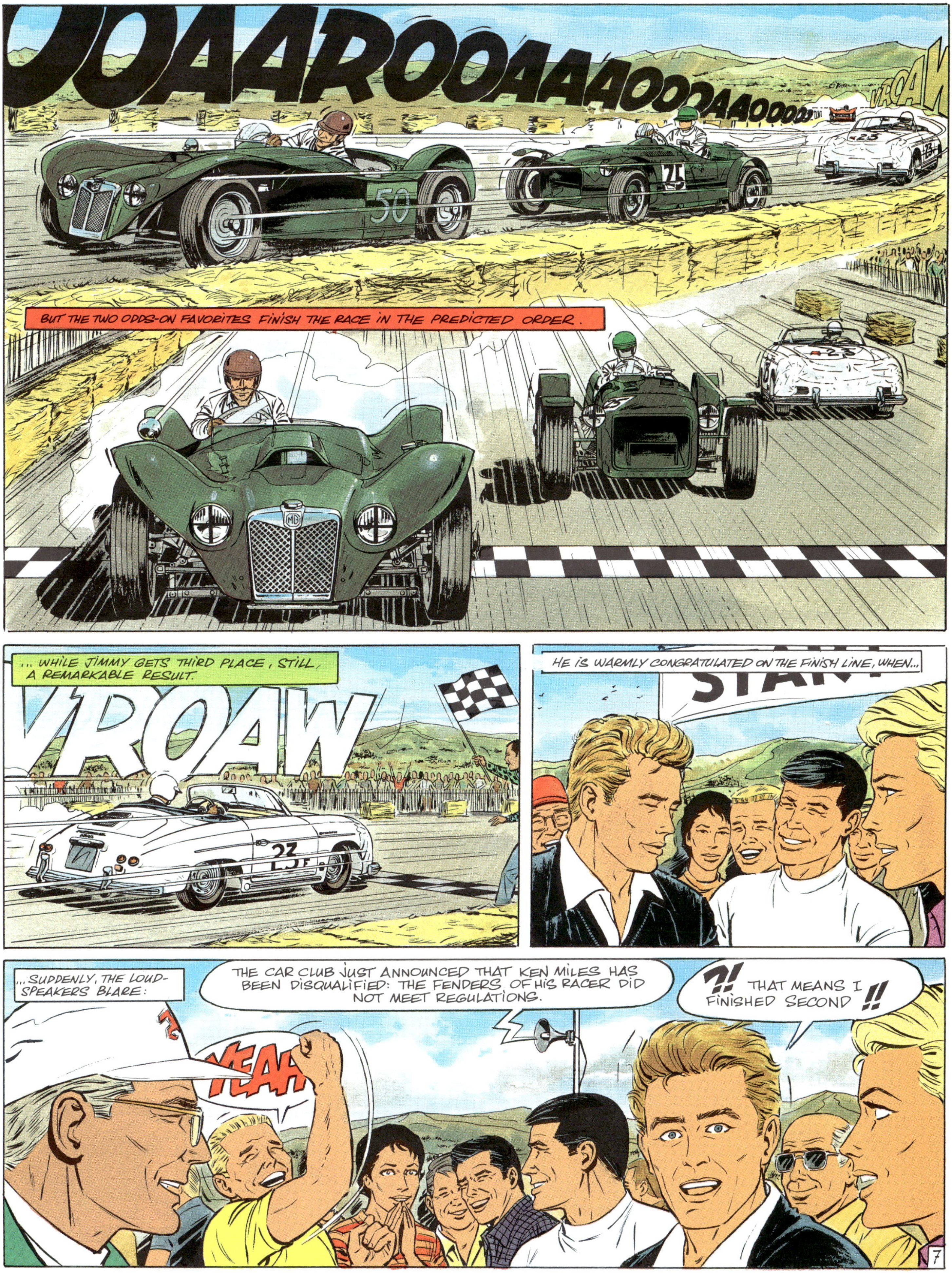

JOAARROOAAAOOOAAOOOO VROAW

BUT THE TWO ODDS-ON FAVORITES FINISH THE RACE IN THE PREDICTED ORDER.

...WHILE JIMMY GETS THIRD PLACE, STILL A REMARKABLE RESULT.

VROAW

HE IS WARMLY CONGRATULATED ON THE FINISH LINE, WHEN...

...SUDDENLY, THE LOUDSPEAKERS BLARE:

THE CAR CLUB JUST ANNOUNCED THAT KEN MILES HAS BEEN DISQUALIFIED: THE FENDERS OF HIS RACER DID NOT MEET REGULATIONS.

?! THAT MEANS I FINISHED SECOND!!

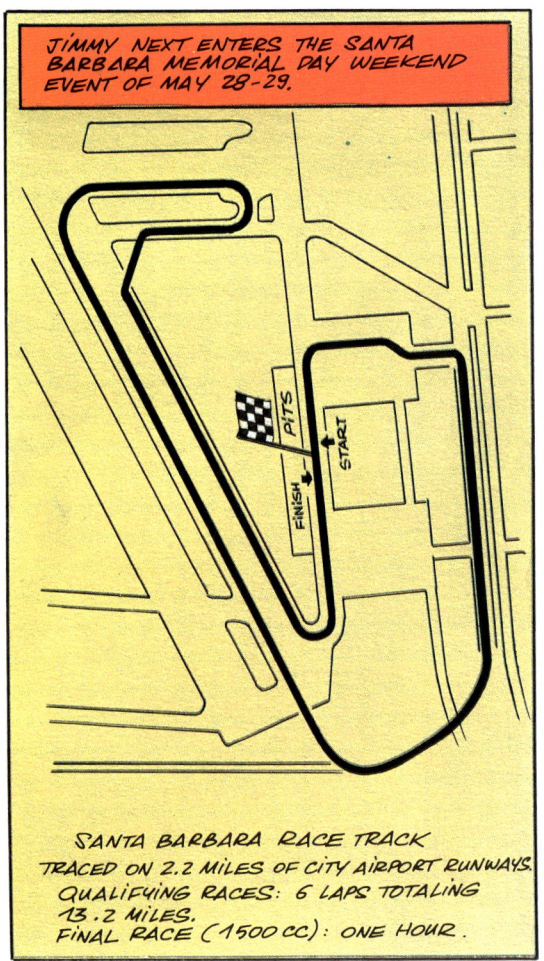

...JIMMY FEELS A STEEP DROP IN POWER. A PISTON HAS MELTED! IN HIS EAGERNESS TO CATCH UP WITH THE MORE POWERFUL CARS, HE OVERSTRESSED HIS ENGINE.

THERE GOES THE WEEKEND!

THE PORSCHE IS TOWED BACK TO THE IMPORTER, COMPETITION MOTORS, FOR REPAIRS.

JIMMY ENTRUSTS IT TO ROLF WÜTHERICH, WHOM HE MET AT BAKERSFIELD. A PORSCHE EMPLOYEE, ROLF IS VON NEUMANN'S BEST MECHANIC AND JIMMY LIKES HIM.

THEN HE TELLS VON NEUMANN:

I WISH I HAD A CAR THAT CAN WIN THE BIG RACES!

THE PRODUCTION OF "REBEL" BEING OVER, JIMMY NOW GOES TO TEXAS TO START WORK ON "GIANT."

A Passion

James Dean was killed on September 30, 1955, while driving to his fourth race. He was only 24 years old. Despite his death, Jimmy's admirers continued to write him more letters than any living actor ever received. Some refused to accept the truth, still believing that their idol was alive, disfigured and hiding from the world. One of the great legends of U.S. film history had just been spawned by a collision between two cars. The "crazy rebel" driver was quickly held responsible. Rightly or wrongly?
The following will shed some light on what was, in reality, a clash between two worlds.

for Speed

It was September 30, 1955, a Friday. As an orange sun dipped behind the Sierras, it highlighted the smile on Jimmy's face. In the narrow cockpit of his brand new Porsche 550 Spyder, Jimmy sped north toward the San Joachin Valley, leaving Hollywood in the far distance. The September air was clear and cool. The streamlined little racer was slicing through it smoothly, its engine humming at 6000 rpm.

Free Again

Dean had just finished shooting Giant, his third feature film. The production company, unwilling to take any risks with the young star, had Jimmy agree to a contract clause forbidding him to race while the film was being made. But now that the contract had been fulfilled, Jimmy was free again to

> This is the film taken by the photographer Sandy Roth, who was following Jimmy in the Ford Station Wagon. It shows the last picture taken of James Dean alive, content at the wheel of his new Spyder. In the next frame, the body of the young actor is loaded into the ambulance.
> Sandy Roth had the discretion not to photograph James Dean's corpse in the wreck of the Spyder. In the next scenes, the ambulance attendants attend to Rolf Wütherich, who was seriously injured but survived.

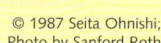

© 1987 Seita Ohnishi;
Photo by Sanford Roth

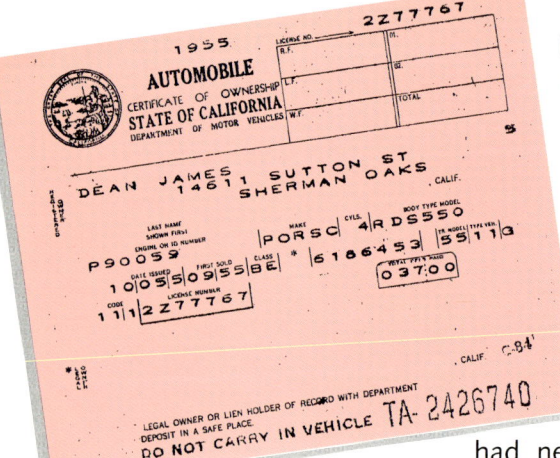

Owner's Certificate (Pink Slip) for James Dean's Porsche.

indulge his true passion: racing sports cars.

James Dean had traded in his Speedster and paid $3,000 to acquire a brand new Spyder 550. It was a rocket compared to the 356 Porsche he had driven during his first three races. New, the car cost $6,900. Jimmy had never owned anything as expensive. He had the number 130 painted on the hood, engine cover, and doors. Then, well in keeping with his rebel image, he had the nickname, "Little Bastard"—a name given to him by a friend—inscribed on the trunk.

From his seat on the passenger side, James Dean's mechanic, Rolf Wütherich, observed the dials on the dashboard. Jimmy had negotiated for Wütherich's services as part of the terms of his purchase of the new Porsche. Race car driver John Von Neumann, the owner of Competition Motors, the Porsche dealership in Hollywood, agreed to Jimmy's request to have Wütherich, the shop's expert

German mechanic, at each of his races. The 28-year-old Wütherich was the best Porsche mechanic in America, having been trained in Stuttgart. Dean, who had befriended Wütherich, had a high regard for his skills.

A Rare Aristocracy

This friendship was characteristic of Jimmy. Hollywood people who knew the German considered him a mere mechanic who hardly spoke English. But Jimmy thought Wütherich belonged to a rare aristocracy: the small circle of experts trained in the maintenance of advanced, complex engines and in the fine art of tuning them for maximum racing performance. Jimmy admired this exceptional talent and hoped to learn much from Wütherich. The German valued Jimmy's appreciation highly and, thus, had spared no effort in preparing the brand new Spyder for its first race. On the road to Salinas, he kept providing Jimmy with counsel, while checking the instrument panel. Both driver and car were working harmoniously.

There were two other people traveling with Dean and Wütherich. Following the Porsche a few car lengths behind was a white Ford Country station wagon towing an empty trailer. Driving the Ford was Bill Hickman, 35, a Hollywood car stuntman. Jimmy had met Hickman during the shooting of *Rebel Without a Cause*. The young actor had immediately noticed Hickman's expertise at controlling automobiles through the most incredible maneuvers. They had become fast friends, and Hickman had been teaching Jimmy advanced racing techniques. Accompanying Hickman in the Ford was Sandy Roth, 38, a well-known Hollywood photographer. Roth had chosen the race weekend in Salinas to complete a photo essay on Jimmy for Collier's. They had met on the set of Giant.

Seated on the Road

The four men were suddenly startled by the sound of a blaring siren. A California Highway Patrol black and white, with lights flashing, rushed in between the two cars. Jimmy was driving at 65 mph, 10 mph over the speed limit. The officer, Otie Hunter, got out of his car and headed toward the Porsche, which didn't resemble anything he had ever seen. The Spyder's hood reached only to his knees, giving the impression that its occupants were seated on the road. After checking the papers and asking about this unusual car, the officer wrote out a ticket for Dean and then Hickman, without realizing who the Porsche driver was. Both cars then continued on their way to the town of Paso Robles, where Jimmy had planned to have a quick meal before driving the remaining 90 miles to Salinas.

Two hours later, after a brief stop at Blackwell's Corners, Jimmy was headed west on a long downhill straightaway near the tiny town of Cholame. As he approached a minor intersection branching off to the his right, Jimmy noticed a black and white Ford veering gradually toward the middle of the road.

Jimmy's new Spyder is delivered to him at Competition Motors. Notice the Beetles and Speedsters, one of which had to be Jimmy's.

"He'll See Us."

The eastbound car seemed to initiate a left turn toward Route 41, which would take it straight across Jimmy's westbound lane. The moment Jimmy noticed this unlikely possibility, he lifted his right foot and veered slightly to the right, hoping to give the other driver more room—or time—to correct his mistake. But the lumbering black and white car kept encroaching further and further across Jimmy's path.

He lifted his right foot instantly and told Wütherich: "That guy up there's gotta stop, he'll see us." These would be James Dean's last words. The following illustrations by Jean Graton recreate the key moments of Jimmy's last day and last moments. They are based on lengthy research including all police photos and reports, witness testimony, and all subsequent analyses by experts. These documents also establish who was to blame for the crash. This is important because in 1955 James Dean was so plagued by the "crazy driver" label that the press uniformly held him responsible for the accident. Any remaining doubts were removed when several witnesses confirmed that he was "driving very fast" and that earlier the same afternoon he had received a speeding ticket. Further compounding his seeming guilt was the "small" size of his "foreign car" with an "irresponsible purpose: racing."

Nonetheless, from the day following the

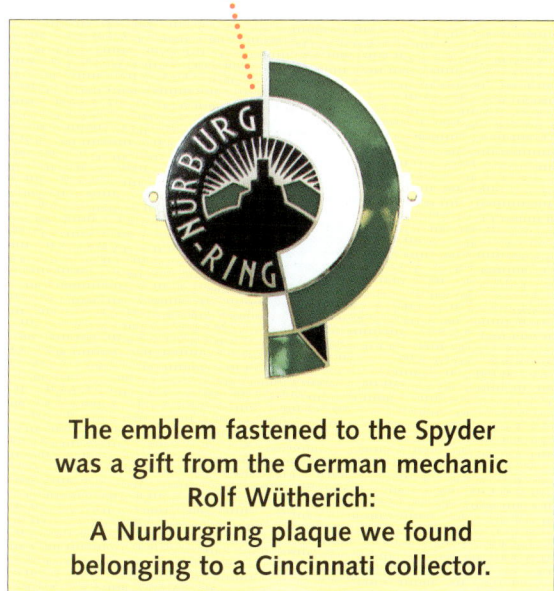

The emblem fastened to the Spyder was a gift from the German mechanic Rolf Wütherich: A Nurburgring plaque we found belonging to a Cincinnati collector.

On September 30, 1955. Jimmy gets ready to drive away. Behind him in the Ford Station Wagon are Hickman and Roth.

Leaving Los Angeles early afternoon on Friday, September 30, 1955.

collision, the basic facts concerning the accident were objectively published. The Los Angeles Mirror News ran this Page One banner headline: "Film Star Killed in Crash." It went on to report: "The California Highway Patrol said a car driven by Donald Turnupseed, 23,...turned left off Highway 466 onto Highway 41 and collided almost head-on with Dean's car."

However, in an adjacent column, the newspaper's Entertainment editor, Dick Williams, wrote: "A Warner Brothers executive who used to see Dean zoom out of the studio with his fast foreign racing car, declared, 'This crazy kid is going to kill himself.' Last night his prophecy came true as one of the most brilliant newcomers I've discovered on the Hollywood scene was killed in his white Porsche in a highway accident near Paso Robles." Williams was even wrong on the color of the car.

Turnupseed Found Innocent

At a hearing in mid-October, a San Luis Obispo jury quickly declared Turnupseed innocent on all counts. It took only two hours for the witnesses and Turnupseed to be questioned and for the jury to reach a decision. The Sheriff and the young prosecutor based all their questioning on two premises. One, that Jimmy's foreign car was quite small and unsafe ("it didn't have a roof."). And, two, that Jimmy was driving much too fast. The court found Turnupseed, a young community resident and member of the local establishment, a new father, and a military veteran, not at fault when he entered Highway 41 from the left and that he simply "didn't see the Porsche."

The legend of James Dean skyrocketed after his death. Following the release of *Rebel Without a Cause* two weeks later, his circle of fans became enormous. It grew further a year later when Giant was released. By late 1956, James Dean had become a myth of major proportions, of which his death was an integral part. And thus, ironically, he reached his ultimate goal, which he once confided to a friend: "If a man can bridge the gap between life and death, if he can live on after he's died...to me the only success, the only greatness...is in immortality."

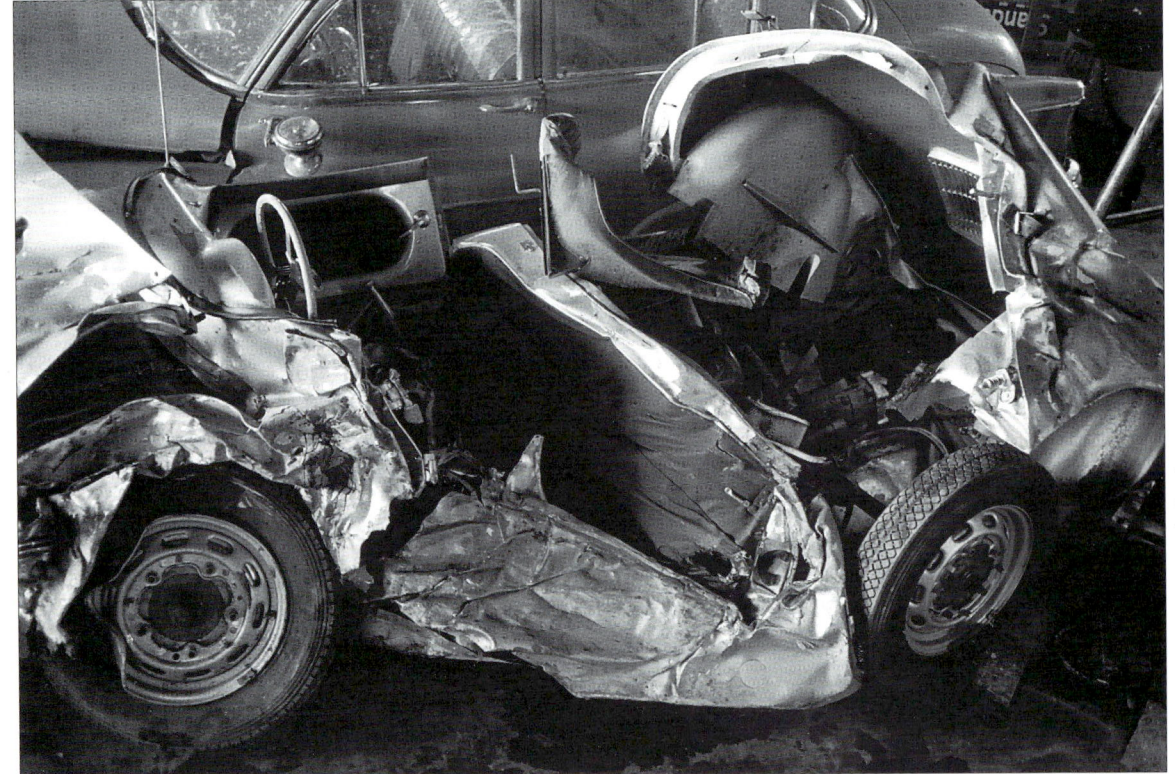

The wreck of the Spyder, photographed in a garage several hours after the tragedy.

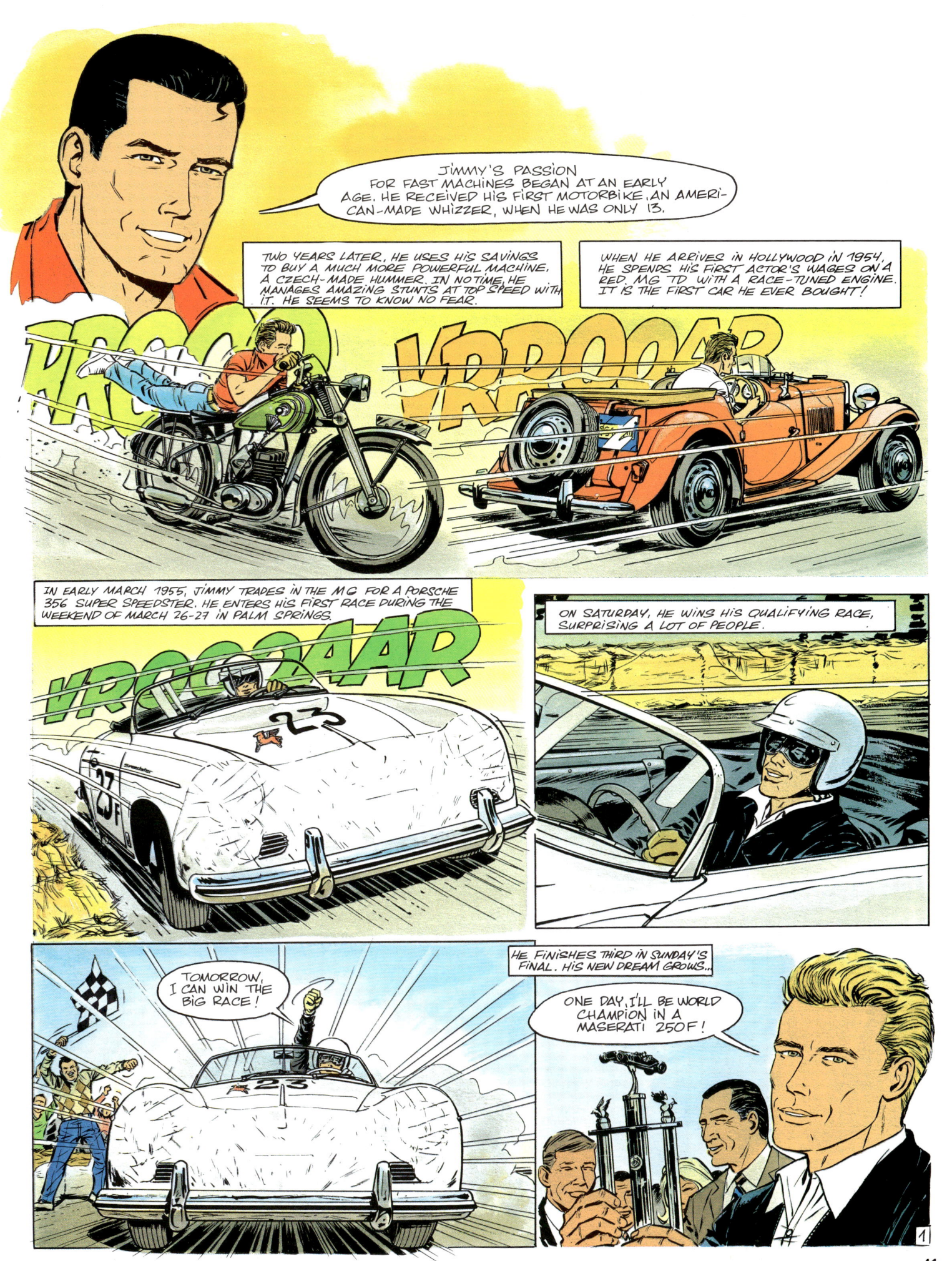

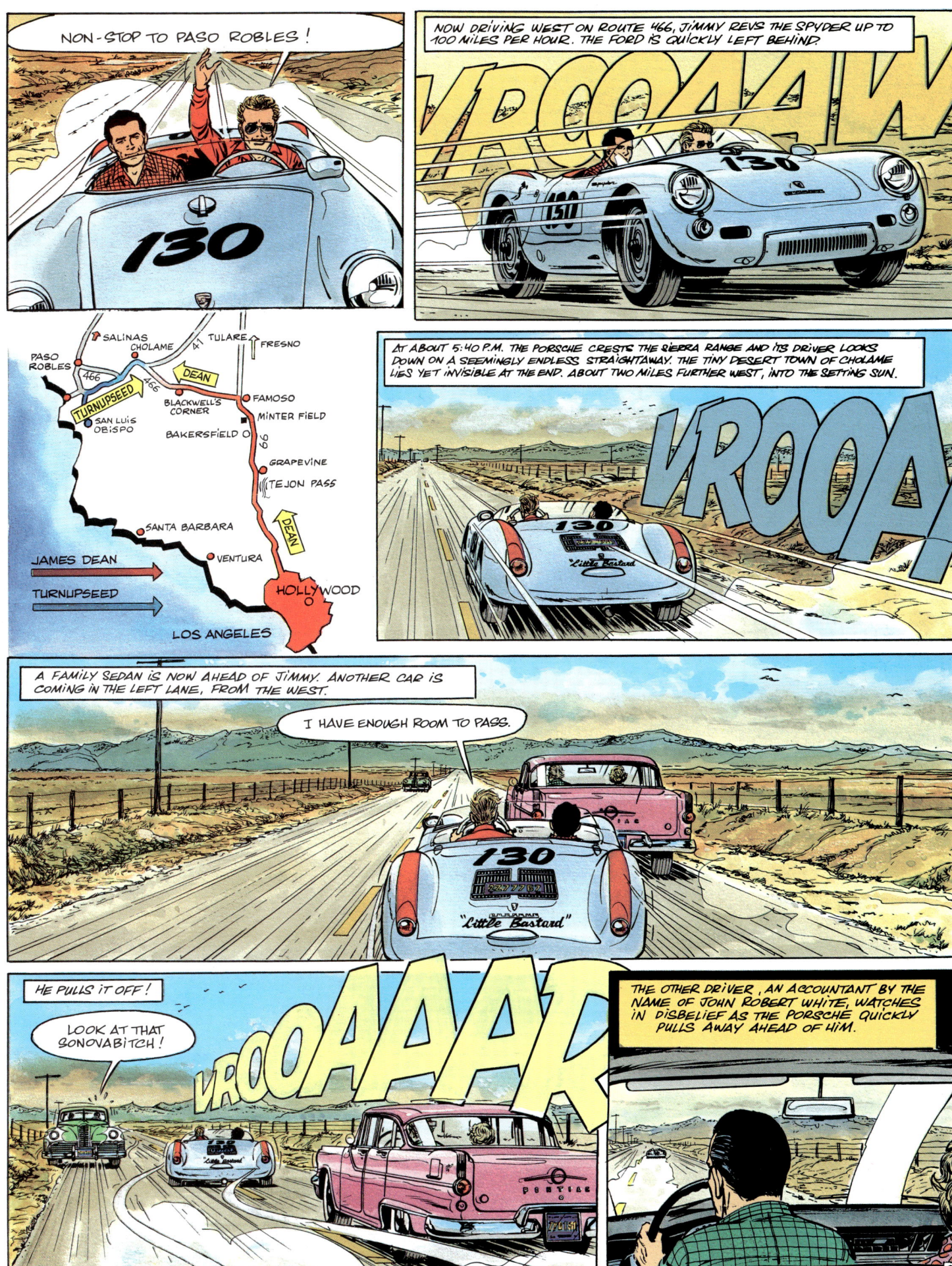

WÜTHERICH, FLUNG FROM HIS SEAT, LIES NEAR THE SMASHED SPYDER, HIS LEFT LEG CRUSHED AND HIS JAW BROKEN. JIMMY LIES SIDEWAYS ACROSS THE COCKPIT, BLEEDING BADLY AND SHOWING NO SIGNS OF LIFE. IT IS 5:45 P.M.

A FEW MINUTES LATER, HICKMAN AND ROTH, THEN AN AMBULANCE, ARRIVE AT THE SCENE, JOINING JOHN ROBERT WHITE AND HIS WIFE. TURNUPSEED, DAZED BUT HAVING SUFFERED NOTHING WORSE THAN A BLOODY NOSE, WATCHES AS JIMMY'S BODY IS FREED FROM THE WRECK AND LAID ON A STRETCHER.

UNCONSCIOUS AND SUFFERING FROM MULTIPLE FRACTURES, INCLUDING OF THE NECK, JIMMY IS ABOUT TO BE RUSHED TO WARD MEMORIAL HOSPITAL IN PASO ROBLES. THERE THE DOCTOR ON DUTY, DR. BOSSERT, WILL DECLARE HIM "DEAD ON ARRIVAL."

JIMMY'S DEATH MAKES HEADLINES THE NEXT DAY...

THUS, A YOUNG MAN WAS KILLED AND A MYTH WAS BORN. THE FOLLOWING WEEK, "REBEL WITHOUT A CAUSE", JIMMY'S SECOND MOVIE, REACHED NATIONAL DISTRIBUTION. MILLIONS OF YOUNG PEOPLE AROUND THE WORLD WOULD SEE IT, LOVE IT AND MOURN ITS STAR. IT WAS THE BEGINNING OF A LEGEND THAT WOULD LIVE FOREVER.

Jean Graton

The Truth

In order to provide an exact reconstruction of this accident, all available witness depositions as well as California Vehicle Accident Report No. 00116, written on September 30, 1955 by officers Nelson and Tripke, were reviewed.

On that Friday evening, Highway 466 was far from empty; there were several witnesses to the accident. Based on what they saw, as well as the police reports examining the cars and the remains of the accident, it is evident that the assumption Jimmy was at fault was premature. However, American newspapers and the American public persisted in this opinion. James Dean was a rebel who challenged the status quo and traditional morality. Donald Turnupseed, the driver of the Ford, was a young man from a good family who was returning home to his pregnant wife following a week of college classes. Jimmy was driving a foreign-German-racing vehicle. (WWII had only ended ten years earlier). Donald had bought an all-American car, a Ford Custom. That same afternoon, Jimmy had been cited for speeding. And shortly before the accident, witnesses saw him driving "recklessly."

THE FACTS

The Ford, coming in the opposite direction, blocked the Porsche's lane by turning left toward Highway 41.

•

The Ford's driver didn't signal.

•

At the moment of impact, the Ford was in the middle of Jimmy's lane.

•

Donald Turnupseed, driver of the Ford, had to see the Porsche coming.

•

Dean was at the wheel at the time of the accident.

Dean's Right of Way

The truth is another story. Traveling in the opposite direction, Turnupseed crossed into Jimmy's lane while turning left. He veered toward the left well ahead of the intersection, without signaling, and when the collision occurred, he was right in the middle of the westbound lane.

Jimmy was not speeding "recklessly" as he approached the intersection. An important study established the speed of the Porsche at the time of impact at somewhere between 55 and 60 mph. If the Porsche had been traveling any faster, it would have landed much further than 45 feet from the point of impact. The photograph on page 48 gives the impression that the Porsche came to a stop when it hit a telephone pole, but this wasn't what happened. The right

The photo shows the spot where the Spyder came to rest after the accident. Route 41, the road Donald Turnupseed was turning into, is seen in the background. Turnupseed, dazed and in shock, is the man in the black T-shirt.

reconstructed

Turnupseed's Ford as seen following the impact. His skid marks are at the center of Jimmy's lane. At the far left, a portion of the white stopping line where Highway 41 flows into Highway 466.

side of the Porsche was intact, and the wooden telephone pole didn't have a scratch on it. Apart from the Ford, the Porsche didn't hit anything. The car's cartwheels absorbed most of the kinetic energy before it came to a stop.

Dean's driving was not at fault. The moment he realized that the Ford wasn't going to turn back into its own lane, he didn't apply the brakes, which would have caused him to lose control of the car. (In an official statement made by the Whites, both said that the Porsche's brake lights never came on.)

Dean's reaction was that of an experienced driver—he lifted his foot from the gas pedal and turned slightly to the right to allow the Ford maximum room to clear him on the left. Alas!...

There were other versions of the incident. Some speculated that Turnupseed didn't even see the Porsche coming, as it was so low riding and the same color as the road. Others even suggested that Wütherich was driving and Dean was the passenger. As is the case in all tragic events, there are many versions of the story. It is very likely that Turnupseed saw the Porsche, as it was visible against the highway from more than 650 yards away. This was confirmed by Turnupseed's skid marks. And the fact that Jimmy's feet were jammed under the pedals, something that delayed the ambulance attendants from removing his body from the Porsche, makes it highly unlikely that he could have been in the passenger seat.

DID YOU KNOW THAT...

...two weeks prior to his death, James Dean starred in a highway safety TV spot. In an interview with Gig Young, Jimmy encouraged young people to exercise caution while driving. He ended by saying, "The life you save could be mine!"

Michael Valliant's Opinion

James Dean: Reckless driver or genuine race car driver?

What should one think of this complex young man who brought a revolutionary new style to Hollywood, then became a legend after a tragic, early death? Was James Dean a troubled youth with a death wish or was he a racing champion in the making?

I know great racing drivers; I have met many during my career. James Dean could have been one of them. Gus Vignolle, a racing journalist who witnessed two of Jimmy's races in the Speedster S, wrote: "His cornering ability with this type of car called for perfect coordination of throttle, brakes and gear shift." Ken Miles said that he "had never before seen such a latent skill in any driver."

James Dean's racing career, though quite short, was that of a true professional. Jimmy had enormous talent, and his early results bear that out. He possessed all the qualities necessary to succeed in this demanding and difficult sport, including a great fighting spirit. Jimmy's most intense passion was focused on racing cars. I believe I know how happy he must have been that late afternoon of September 30, 1955, steering his new Porsche Spyder, zooming down the long, straight road. I know that joy; I share that same passion. But no passion nor rebellious spirit justifies losing one's life so early.

Beyond the question of who was to blame, what concerns me most are the unnecessary losses. While Wütherich survived, he returned to Germany deeply shaken by the experience. After a series of business failures and four marriages, he died on July 20, 1981, when his car crashed into a wall in his native town of Kupferzell. Donald Turnupseed, who continued to live in Tulare, died in the summer of 1995. Although he had refused to speak to anybody about that tragic evening some 40 years before, it would not be surprising to learn that he thought about it nearly every day.

James Dean died of multiple fractures and severe trauma. That is the troubling part. Life is not a movie; you can't shout, "Cut," then reshoot the last scene.

THE CAUSE OF MR. OHNISHI

A remarkable Japanese man devotes his life to the memory of James Dean, including building actual monuments...

Mr. Ohnishi is the most surprising collector of James Dean photos and documents. His interest is not commercial. When he bought the negatives and copyrights for the last pictures taken of his idol, it was not to turn a future profit but to make sure those pictures would never be used in a less than honorable way. One of his concerns was to verify if the photographer Sandy Roth, after arriving at the accident site, had taken any pictures of James Dean dying. Here is what Seita Ohnishi has to say (see pictures on pages 36-37: "In answer to my question: 'Did your husband photograph Jimmy's death mask at Cholame,' Sandy's widow, who kindly assisted me in establishing the monument at Cholame, answered: 'My husband did not take the photograph.' A few years later, when all the negatives and copyrights for Jimmy were transferred to me by Sandy's widow, I confirmed that it was true." Seita Ohnishi lives in Kobe, Japan. That city was ravaged by a terrifying earthquake in 1995 just at the time we were trying to obtain the negatives taken by Sandy Roth. In spite of the circumstances—Mr. Ohnishi was helping supply Kobe survivors with fresh water—he sent us the requested material in a timely way after making sure of the intention of our book. We were touched by this gesture, and we wish to thank him for his confidence in us.

1. Monument erected by Seita Ohnishi at Cholame, near the collision site.

2. James Dean attending a Kendo ceremony.

3. The La Coste sculpture. Seita Ohnishi commissioned this work to honor James Dean and as a gift to the American people. In the future, after the best spot for it has been found, he dreams of having it shipped from La Coste, in the south of France, to the United States.

The Porsches of James Dean

SPEEDSTER 356-1500 SUPER

In 1936, Professor Ferdinand Porsche developed the famous Volkswagen "Beetle". By 1948, his son Ferry decided to use it as the basis for developing the first car to bear the Porsche name: a sports coupe named Type 356. The Porsche 356 quickly found a receptive audience, even in America. Importer Max Hoffman named it the "Speedster". The car was soon seen on numerous American race tracks. It was eventually superseded on road racing circuits by the much faster 550 Spyder, but it remains both a classic and the progenitor of the famed Porsche 911.

ENGINE: 1488cc flat four, type 528/2 (modified from VW). **POWER**: 70 hp @ 5400 rpm. Weight: 1695 lbs. **MAXIMUM SPEED**: 101 mph.

SPYDER 550-1500 RS

Porsche introduced its second model (the 550/1500 RS) at the Paris Auto Salon in 1953. It featured a sophisticated new flat four, four-cam engine.

Max Hoffman later renamed the car "Spyder" for the American market–a name that caught on around the world.

The new racing Porsche quickly proved itself a winning car, finishing first in its class at the Carrera Panamericana Mexico in 1953 and 1954, and fourth overall at Le Mans in 1955.

James Dean's Spyder was built in Zuffenhausen near Stuttgart in 1955, and carried chassis number 550.0055. Although a "street legal" version for the American market, it was a very potent racing machine.

ENGINE: Four-cam Porsche flat-four, type 547. **POWER**: 110 hp @ 6200 rpm. Weight: 1200 lbs. **MAXIMUM SPEED**: 135 mph

Jean Graton was assisted by Jean-Luc Delvaux in preparing the illustrated stories in the book. The individual illustrations on pages 18, 19, 20, and 51 were drawn by Daniel Bouchez. Texts have been written by Philippe Defechereux, Philippe Graton and Michel Thiriar.

The authors would like to thank the following people for their invaluable assistance: Steve Marmon and David Chu of New York, for their support throughout the project; Jim Sitz, California racing reporter, who saw James Dean's first two races; and Lee Raskin, Baltimore lawyer, member of the Porsche Club of America and well-known historian of the two Porsches owned by James Dean. The authors would like to thank the following people for their help and the technical consultation they provided: Roland D'Ieteren, Jacques Swaters and Etienne Visart.

BIBLIOGRAPHY

American Road Race Specials	Allan Girdler	1990
Blessing in Disguise	Alec Guinness	1986
Classic Porsche Racing Cars	Michael Cotton	1988
Lotus–The Sports Racing Cars	Anthony Pritchard	1987
Porsche–Speedster	Michel Thiriar	1995
Porsche–Excellence was Expected	Karl Ludvigsen	1977
Porsche 356 &550–A Pictorial History	Henry Rasmussen	1992
Porsche 356 & RS Spyders	Gordon Maltby	1991
Power Behind the Wheel	Walter J. Boyne	1988
Scarab	Preston Lerner	1991
The American Automobile–A Centerary	G. N. Georgano	1992
The Concise Dictionary of Motorsport	George Bishop	1979
The Encyclopedia of Motorsport	G. N. Georgano	1971
Vintage Motorsports	Issues 5 and 6	1992
Boulevard of Broken Dreams	Paul Alexander	1994
James Dean	Barney Hoskyns	1994
James Dean–American Icon	David Dalton	1984
James Dean–Behind the Scenes	L. Adams/K. Burns	1990
James Dean–Little Boy Lost	Joe Hyams	1992
James Dean–The Memory of the Last 85 Days	S. Roth/Seita Ohnishi	1987
James Dean Revisited	Dennis Stock	1987
James Dean–Tribute to a Rebel	Val Holley	1991
The Death of James Dean	Warren N. Beath	1986
The Fifties	David Halberstam	1993
The Mutant King	David Dalton	1974
The Unabridged James Dean	Randall Riese	1989

«WE REMEMBER DEAN CLUB»

The **We Remember Dean International** (WRDI) fan club is the best known and most active James Dean commemorative club. For the past 15 years, **Sylvia Bongiovanni**, co-founder and current president of the club, has been the driving force behind it. Located in California, WRDI maintains a large collection of original photos and articles, books, magazines, records, and historical objects related to Jimmy. WRDI publishes a bi-monthly newsletter reporting all activities worldwide dedicated to James Dean. The newsletter is sent to all club members. WRDI and Sylvia invite new members to join. Write:

We Remember Dean International
P. O. Box 5025 - Fullerton, CA 92635 - U.S.A.

«JAMES DEAN GALLERY»

The most complete museum dedicated to James Dean is located in Fairmount, Indiana, Jimmy's boyhood home. A 12-room house is the site of **The James Dean Gallery** and its impressive collection of items owned by the young actor, including clothing and drawings and paintings he did himself. The museum's owner and founder is **David Loehr**, a New Yorker who was inspired by the legend in 1974 after seeing East of Eden. In addition to overseeing the museum, David Loehr organizes other events related to preserving the memory of Jimmy, the best known of which is the annual "Tour of New York places frequented by James Dean."

The James Dean Gallery
P. O. Box 55 - Fairmount, IN 46928 - U.S.A.